Animals of the World
Consultant Editor Sir Maurice Yonge CBE FRS

Chimpanzees

Ralph Whitlock

Contents

1	Apes and Monkeys	5
2	The Chimpanzee Clans	15
3	The Day Dawns	25
4	Family Life	39
5	The Future of the Chimpanzee	47
	Glossary	54
	Further Reading	56
	Index	57

RAINTREE CHILDRENS BOOKS
Milwaukee ● Toronto ● Melbourne ● London

First published in the United States of America by Raintree
Publishers Limited, 1977.

Distributed to the Book Trade by the Two Continents
Publishing Group, 30 East 42nd Street, New York, 10017

Library of Congress Number: 77-13965

1 2 3 4 5 6 7 8 9 0 81 80 79 78 77

Printed in England by Loxley Brothers Ltd.
Library bound in the United States of America.

First published in the United Kingdom by
Wayland Publishers Ltd., 1977.

Library of Congress Cataloging in Publication Data

Whitlock, Ralph.
   Chimpanzees.

   (Animals of the World)

   Bibliography: p. 56.
   Includes index.
   SUMMARY: Introduces the monkey family, particularly the
wild chimpanzees of the central African forests.
   1. Chimpanzees—Juvenile literature.   [1 .
Chimpanzees].   I. Title.
QL737.P96W48 1977   55'.884   77-13965
ISBN 0-8172-1077-6 lib. bdg.

Paperback edition ISBN 0-8467-0400-5

Introduction

In every zoo, the apes and monkeys attract big crowds. After all, they are our closest animal relatives. The chimpanzee is about as smart as a four-year-old child. It can use sticks to dig for food and stones to hunt small animals. When eating it can use leaves as we use spoons. It can "talk" with its own special language of signs and sounds. Sometimes it will sit holding hands with a friend. Illustrated throughout with color photographs, this book takes us to meet members of the ape and monkey family, and into the world of the wild chimpanzees that live in the central African forests.

**1
Apes and Monkeys**

Which animals are most like human beings? They are the ape and the many species of monkey. Most monkeys live in trees and have hands and feet made for grasping branches. They have flattened faces, like ours. Their eyes are set close together at the front, so that both look in the same direction. Their eyesight is their main help in the fight for survival.

Marmosets are in the same animal group as monkeys. They are small, furry, long-clawed animals that live in the treetops of South American forests.

The picture below is of another South American monkey, the red uakari. It has a red face and no hair and looks like a bald old man.

The red uakari shares its forest home with spider monkeys. These have very long arms and legs, which make them look like spiders clambering about in the trees. Many of them have prehensile (grasping) tails. They use this as an extra hand to help them swing through the trees.

In Africa and Asia, too, there are many monkeys that live in trees. Others prefer to roam the plains. They run around on all fours, like dogs. Some of them, such as the baboons, have long snouts and look a little like dogs. One species, the patas monkey, often stands upright to look over the long grass. When doing so, it uses its long tail for balance.

The strange-looking animal on the right is the proboscis monkey. It lives in the forests of Borneo and eats leaves and fruit. Young proboscis monkeys look like other monkeys, but as they grow older their nose grows larger and longer until it is quite huge. Scientists believe that it acts as a sounding board for the monkey's voice.

The ape family includes the gorilla, the chimpanzee, the orangutan (left), and six kinds of gibbon. All of them live in tropical forests. The gibbons and the orangutan live in Southeast Asia; the gorilla and chimpanzee live in Africa. Gibbons are long-armed apes that swing from branch to branch in the treetops. The white-banded gibbon (above) lives in Thailand. It lives almost entirely in trees, seldom coming down to the ground. Its arms are very strong. It can leap as far as 15 m. (50 ft.) from one branch to another. It can easily support its weight by grasping a branch with one hand.

Chimpanzees and orangutans are equally at home on the ground or in trees. Gorillas (above) are so large and heavy that they spend most of their time on the ground. They have to—many tree branches are not strong enough to support their weight!

In this book we are going to look at chimpanzees and the life they lead in their jungle home. The chimpanzee is the best-loved member of the ape family. Perhaps this is because it behaves more like us than any other ape or monkey, as you will see.

2
The
Chimpanzee Clans

Most people have seen chimpanzees in a zoo. Most chimps in zoos, however, are young ones that are not nearly as big as adults. An adult male chimpanzee measures up to $1\frac{1}{2}$ m. (5 ft.) tall when standing erect, and weighs as much as 55 kg. (120 lb.).

The chimpanzee is covered with long, blackish hair, except for the face and hands, which are bare. It has ears like those of humans, except that chimps' are larger and stick out. Chimpanzees have no tail. They are among the most intelligent of animals. In some ways they act like human beings, and they can be taught to mimic us. They are, in fact, about as intelligent as a four-year-old child. In their wild state they have learned to use several types of tools.

Sometimes chimpanzees make faces that we think we understand. Often we are wrong. The chimpanzee's expressions and gestures have a meaning of their own, as we shall see later.

The natural home of the chimpanzee is the forest zone of central Africa, from Uganda to the west coast. In large parts of that vast area, however, it is now extinct. Even so, it has a range of over $2\frac{1}{2}$ million sq. km. (1 million sq. mi.). Some chimpanzees live in the middle of dense forests, but most prefer to live on the edge of the forest. This is because they like to go searching for food in the clearings and plains during the day and return to the trees for safety at night. They also like hilly country, perhaps because they can see their enemies better from the tops of trees growing on hills. Then they can escape quickly into the jungle.

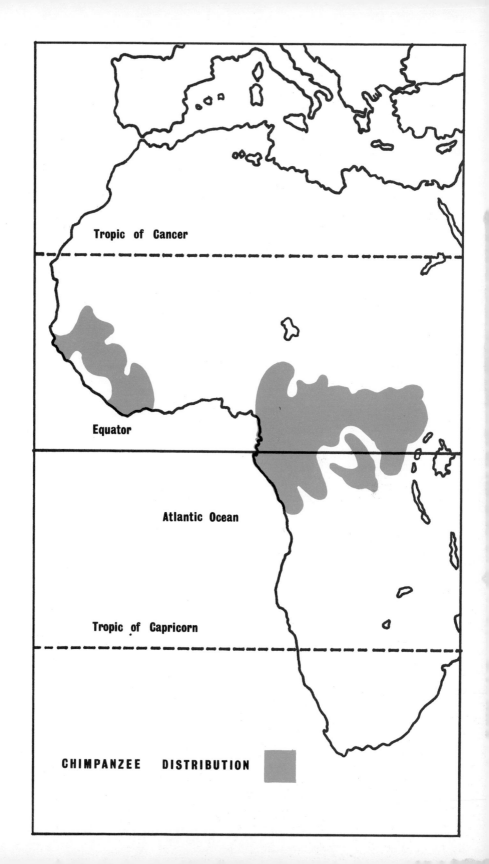

Tropic of Cancer

Equator

Atlantic Ocean

Tropic of Capricorn

CHIMPANZEE DISTRIBUTION

Chimpanzees like to live in groups. They form clans of as many as 60 or 80 animals. The heart of the clan consists of a group of females with their young. The males and young adults are loosely attached to this group. Often they go off on their own, especially when food is scarce. Each clan wanders over an area of about 20 to 25 sq. km. (8 to 10 sq. mi.) in forest country, or up to 80 sq. km. (30 sq. mi.) in savannah country. (Savannah is a grassy plain with scattered groups of trees.)

There is a main, or dominant, male in each clan, but he does not get his position by fighting for it. Chimpanzees hardly ever fight. From time to time a group of males meets for a shouting match. The one who shouts loudest and makes the most fuss is accepted as leader. The others show him some respect but will move out of his way rather than argue with him.

Chimpanzees are not natural fighters. In any conflict, they would much rather run away than fight. Their displays are very much a matter of form.

The territories of different chimpanzee clans often overlap. When two clans meet they either ignore each other or behave in a friendly manner. They do not fight. Sometimes chimpanzees will switch from one clan to another if they are not happy where they are.

In the chimpanzee's forest home, there is little difference between the seasons. Day and night are always the same in length, and the temperature varies very little. In much of Africa there are two dry seasons and two wet seasons. During

the dry season food becomes scarce, and so the chimpanzee clans have to forage over a wider area. In the great rain-forests, however, where many of the chimpanzees live, heavy rain may fall at any time. Then there is plenty of food.

3
The Day Dawns

The day for chimpanzees begins at dawn. In the tropics day and night are of equal length, so the chimpanzee clan spends twelve hours sleeping and twelve hours moving about. By daybreak the animals are hungry. As soon as they wake up, they go foraging, sometimes in the treetops and sometimes on the ground. After a few hours of activity, they often rest in the middle of the day and go foraging again for an hour or two before sunset.

When searching for food, the clan splits up into smaller bands. Some bands are made up of chimpanzees of both sexes, some of mothers and their young and some of males of all ages. Sometimes males also move around on their own.

The chimpanzee is mainly vegetarian, although it has a wide range of diet. For much of the time it finds plenty of fruit to eat in the forests. It also eats the leaves, bark, and pith, or core, of trees. On the forest floor it will dig for roots and tubers. For animal protein it eats ants, termites, and other insects. It will also rob birds' nests and kill small animals, including other monkeys. In times of scarcity a group will combine to attack and kill larger or stronger animals, such as wild pigs, baboons, and antelopes. When a kill has been made, the males call other foraging chimpanzee bands to come and join the feast. Chimpanzees are always willing to share whatever food is available.

In the wild, chimpanzees seldom drink. When we see them drinking from cups in the chimpanzees' tea-party at the zoo, their behavior is quite unnatural. Normally they quench their thirst by eating juicy food. When they do need to drink, they dip their hands into water and lick them. Sometimes they dip crushed leaves into water and suck them.

When a chimpanzee uses leaves as a kind of sponge or spoon, that is an example of using a tool. Chimpanzees will also push and probe with sticks, to dig for roots or scrape insects from their hiding places. They use sticks and stones as weapons when hunting wild game. A common trick is to push a stick into a nest of ants or termites. The insects swarm all over the stick, and the chimpanzee picks them off with its lips. In inviting other members of the clan to come and feast on a newly discovered food supply, male chimpanzees will sometimes beat on a tree trunk with a stick. In zoos we can often see chimpanzees using a stick to reach tidbits that are out of reach of their hands.

Chimpanzees "talk" to each other by means of sound, touch, and sight.

One of their calls is a loud hooting. It can be heard up to 3 km. (2 mi.) away. When a group of chimpanzees finds a new food supply, they sit down and hoot in chorus, to tell the good news to other members of the clan. They also hoot together when they are displaying, or showing off, to see which male is going to be the leader.

A low hoot is a warning signal. Fear or rage is expressed by loud screams. A loud bark means a threat. Apart from all these sounds, chimpanzees use low grunts when they are "talking" to each other.

Adult chimpanzees often have special friends, sometimes of the same sex as themselves. They fondle and groom each other. Often they hold hands, cuddle, and kiss, like human lovers. Chimpanzees love the feeling of touching each other. It is during these sessions that they use their grunting language.

Chimpanzees also communicate with their faces, as we do. But their expressions do not always mean the same as ours. For instance, what appears to us to be a grin, with both rows of teeth showing between bared lips, is usually a sign of defiance. When the mouth is open with the upper teeth hidden, the chimpanzee is in a friendly mood and is ready to play or caress. When chimpanzees pout their lips, as we can often see them doing in a zoo, it is a sign that they are interested in whatever is going on.

What do you think these two chimpanzees (left and above) are trying to say?

When traveling among the treetops, chimpanzees can swing from branch to branch using their hands the way gibbons do. They only use this method, however, for short distances. Over long distances they prefer to travel on the ground because their arms get too tired swinging in the trees. They run on all fours, with their

fingers curled into their hands, so that the soft palms never touch the ground. Most of their weight rests on their hind legs, and they use their hands just to steady themselves. When climbing large trees, they grasp the trunk with their arms and boost themselves upwards by pressing with their feet.

Monkeys in general have many enemies. Any flesh-eating animal, bird, or reptile that can catch them enjoys their tasty flesh. Leopards are especially dangerous, because they can climb trees. Other tree-climbing enemies are large snakes. On the ground prowl jungle cats, servals, and other catlike creatures. Monkeys that venture onto the open plains run the risk of being caught by cheetahs, hyenas, and wild dogs. Those that go to water holes or rivers to drink may be snatched by crocodiles or, in South America, by alligators. Over the tops of the trees soar eagles and hawks, ready to pounce on anything they see moving. One very large and fierce bird of prey that lives in the Philippines is actually known as the monkey-eating eagle, because monkeys form the chief part of its diet.

Chimpanzees and the other large apes have fewer enemies than monkeys, because of their greater size. Danger for them comes chiefly from leopards.

4
Family Life

Chimpanzees are fully grown at about six or seven years old. Then the female is old enough to mate.

The gestation period for chimpanzees is eight months, compared with nine months for gorillas, orangutans, and humans. Normally only one young is born at a time. It is helpless and almost hairless. Like human babies, young chimpanzees are slow to mature; it is some time before they are able to fend for themselves. They spend the first three months of their lives being carried about and breast-fed by their mothers. For much of that time the baby is cradled in its mother's arms. When she is moving about with the clan, it clings to her hair, often on her back. The young chimpanzee has a very strong grip.

Rearing and training young chimpanzees is a long process, like training young humans. Like us, chimps have many things to learn. When they are four or five months old, the young chimpanzees start to move around on their own. At first they keep very near their mothers, for protection. Often a chimp holds its mother's hand or just touches her fingers. Their mothers treat them with love and affection.

As they grow older they join play groups with other youngsters in the clan. The adults in the clan will always unite to protect them against enemies. The mothers are as interested in each other's young as in their own. They are quite happy to help to rear and teach them.

The young stay with their mothers and the other females until they are five or six years old. Then the young males form groups of their own and go off on foraging parties. The young females, which are nearly ready to become mothers themselves, stay with the older ones. All the members of the clan come together from time to time, especially for a feast.

Nest-building by chimpanzees has little or nothing to do with breeding or the birth of babies. It is possible that babies are born at night, when the mother is sitting in her nest, but we know very little about this. The nest is really only a place to sleep.

As a rule, each animal makes its own nest, which it stays in for one night only. As dusk falls it builds a platform of broken branches, over which it bends growing twigs to form a roof, or canopy. Other leafy branches are added to make a bed. The nest is quite flimsy. Making it takes only five or ten minutes.

The nests are usually built in rather slender trees, which sway under the weight of the chimpanzees. This may seem a poor choice, but the slender trees do offer protection from the tree-climbing leopard, which is one of the chimpanzee's chief enemies. Sometimes the nests are 30 m. (100 ft.) or more above the ground.

In the morning the chimpanzees leave their nests and do not, as a rule, ever return to them. Sometimes in the rainy season, however, they make daytime nests for shelter from the rain.

5
The Future
of the Chimpanzee

As with most large animals in Africa, the future of the chimpanzee in the wild depends very much on how well the land is looked after. Fortunately, there are now very large reserves for wild animals in most African countries. If the reserves can be kept safe, they will help the animals survive. But the people in Africa need food. More and more of the land that was to be kept for animals is now being used to grow food for humans instead (left). And as the human population increases, so forests are cut down to make fields, from which the chimpanzees are chased away. So the chimpanzee clans are being driven back farther and farther into country where there is sometimes not enough food to support them.

There are now four races of chimpanzee found in Africa. They are:

The Upper Guinea chimpanzee (scientific name *Pan troglodytes verus*), found in what remains of tropical forest country in West Africa, from Senegal to Nigeria.

The Zaire chimpanzee (*Pan troglodytes troglodytes*) (above), found in equatorial Africa north of Zaire.

The pigmy chimpanzee (*Pan troglodytes paniscus*) (right), found in the Zaire rain forests, south of the River Zaire.

The long-coated chimpanzee (*Pan troglodytes schweinfurthii*), found in Uganda and neighboring countries, especially in mountain forests.

There must still be many hundreds of thousands, perhaps millions, of wild chimpanzees in Africa. It will be many years before they are in any danger of extinction. For some other apes and monkeys, the threat of extinction is very real. For instance, there are thought to be no more than about 600 mountain gorillas left in the wild. When an animal becomes as rare as that, it is in another sort of danger. Collectors can sell it for large sums of money to zoos. Sometimes collectors who do not really care about the animals kill the mothers in order to catch the babies, which are easier to keep in captivity.

Some species have suffered in the past by being hunted. The orangutan is now a rare animal, because it has been hunted and captured to be put in zoos. Collecting must be strictly controlled if this animal is not to become extinct.

Zoos, however, have an important part to play in the future of many animals, including the chimpanzee. If all the wild animals were to disappear, chimpanzees could survive through those that are bred in zoos. Chimpanzees breed well in captivity. Most zoos have breeding colonies. From these colonies chimpanzees could, if necessary, be taken to re-stock reserves in their native land. It will be a long time before any such measures will have to be taken with the chimpanzee. With some other members of the ape and monkey families, it could happen very soon.

Glossary

BABOON A monkey with a short tail and a long, doglike face.

CHEETAH One of the largest, fastest and most powerful members of the cat family.

CLAN A group larger than a single family.

DOMINANT MALE The adult male who leads a group of animals. Each chimpanzee clan has one dominant male.

EXTINCT Died out (used to describe an animal or species).

FORAGING Wandering through the countryside searching for food.

GESTATION PERIOD The period between mating and the birth of the baby animal; the period during which the baby develops in its mother's body.

GIBBONS Long-armed apes that live in the forests of Southeast Asia.

GORILLA The largest of all the apes.

HYENA A large, flesh-eating animal that looks like a dog and hunts in packs.

MARMOSETS Small, monkeylike animals that live in tropical America.

ORANGUTAN One of the large apes; it has long arms and foxy-red hair and lives in the forests of Indonesia.

PITH The soft white part of a fruit, between the skin and the flesh.

PREHENSILE Grasping; a word used to describe the tails of certain monkeys that are able to use their tails as a fifth limb.

PROBOSCIS A long nose.

PROTEIN An essential element of food which helps to keep the body healthy.

RAIN FOREST Dense tropical forest, in which heavy rain falls almost daily.

SAVANNAH A region of grassy plains with scattered trees.

SERVAL A catlike animal that lives in Africa.

TERMITES Antlike creatures that live in large underground colonies; also sometimes known as white ants.

TROPICS The area of the world around the Tropic of Cancer and the Tropic of Capricorn.

TUBERS The edible roots of plants.

VEGETARIAN A creature that lives entirely on plants; it does not eat the flesh of other animals.

Further Reading

Alston, Eugenia. *Growing Up Chimpanzees.* New York: Thomas Y. Crowell Company, 1975.

Burton, Maurice, and Burton, Robert, editors. *The International Wildlife Encyclopedia.* 20 vols. Milwaukee: Purnell Reference Books, 1970.

Conklin, Gladys. *Chimpanzee Roams the Forest.* New York: Holiday House, 1970.

D'Aulaire, Emily, and D'Aulaire, Ola. *Chimps and Baboons.* Washington, D.C.: National Wildlife, 1974.

Morris, Dean. *Monkeys and Apes.* Milwaukee: Raintree Childrens Books, 1977.

ACKNOWLEDGMENTS

The author and publisher would like to thank the following for their permission to reproduce copyright illustrations on the pages mentioned: Bruce Coleman, jacket front, endpapers, 14-15, 16, 20, 26, 28, 33, 34, 42, 45, 48 (Helmut Albrecht), 7 (Norman Myers), 9 (Bruce Coleman), 11 (C. B. Frith), 18 (G. D. Plage), 32 (S. C. Bisserot), 43 (Des Bartlett); Ardea London, 24 (John Gooders), 31, 49, 50 (Kenneth W. Fink), 46 (J. L. Mason), 52 (C. Weaver), jacket back (M. E. J. Gore); N.H.P.A., 13, 22-23, 35, 37, 38; Alan Hutchison Library, 6, 40, 53; Frank W. Lane, 4-5, 27; Heather Angel, 10, 12; Eric Hosking, 41; map, p. 19, Michael Paysden.

Index

Africa, 8, 18, 22, 48
Alligator, 36
Asia, 8

Babies, 39, 44, 51
Baboons, 8, 26
Borneo, 8

Calls, 30
Cheetahs, 36
Clans, 21, 25, 43
Collectors, 51, 53
Crocodiles, 36

Displays, 21
Drinking, 29

Eagles, 36
Enemies, 18, 36
Expressions, 17, 33

Food, 23, 26, 29
Foraging, 21, 23, 25, 26, 43
Forests, 18, 21, 22, 23, 26, 47

Game reserves, 47
Gestation period, 39
Gibbons, 11
Gorilla, 11, 12, 39, 51

Hawks, 36
Hunters, 51
Hyenas, 36

Leaders, 21

Leopards, 36, 44

Marmoset, 7
Mating, 39

Nests, 44

Orangutan, 11, 12, 39, 51

Patas monkey, 8
Plains, 8, 18
Proboscis monkey, 8

Rain forests, 23, 48
Red uakari, 7, 8

Savannah, 21
Seasons, 22, 23
Servals, 36
Sleeping, 25
Snakes, 36
South America, 7
Spider monkeys, 8

Tails (prehensile), 8
"Talking", 30
Territory, 21
Tools, 29
Training, 40
Trees, 7, 8, 11, 12, 18, 34, 35

Uganda, 18

Young, 40, 43

Zoos, 17, 29, 51, 53